1 MONTH OF
FREE
READING

at

www.ForgottenBooks.com

By purchasing this book you are eligible for one month membership to ForgottenBooks.com, giving you unlimited access to our entire collection of over 700,000 titles via our web site and mobile apps.

To claim your free month visit:

www.forgottenbooks.com/free212349

ISBN 978-0-265-20735-2
PIBN 10212349

ANNUAL REGISTER

OF THE

UNITED STATES NAVAL ACADEMY

AT

ANNAPOLIS, MD.,

FOR

THE ACADEMIC YEAR 1869-'70.

WASHINGTON:
GOVERNMENT PRINTING OFFICE.
1869.

NAVAL SCHOOL.

FOUNDED OCTOBER 10, 1845.

JAMES K. POLK, *President of the United States.*
GEORGE BANCROFT, *Secretary of the Navy.*

The Naval School was reorganized on the 1st July, 1850, under the title of Naval Academy, as a school of theoretical and practical science. At that time the course of instruction was materially en-larged, and the institution was placed under the supervision of the Chief of the Bureau of Ordnance and Hydrography.

In October, 1851, the present course of instruction of four years was adopted.

On the establishment of the Bureau of Navigation, (July 5, 1862,) the academy was placed under its supervision.

March 1, 1867, it was placed under the direct care and supervision of the Secretary of the Navy, and its departmental administrative routine and financial management conducted through the Bureau of Navigation, in the Navy Department.

Since March 11, 1869, it has been under the direct care and supervision of the Secretary of the Navy.

BOARD OF VISITORS.

The following named gentlemen were invited by the Hon. Secretary of the Navy to attend the exam-ination of the midshipmen of the Naval Academy in May, 1869.

Rear-Admiral HIRAM PAULDING, U. S. N., *President.*
Commodore JOHN R. GOLDSBOROUGH, U. S. N.
JOSEPH R. HAWLEY, of Connecticut.
Captain ENOCH G. PARROTT, U. S. N.
WILLIAM J. ALBERT, of Maryland,
Surgeon WILLIAM M. WOOD, U. S. N.
D. C. HUMPHREYS, of Alabama.
Chief Engineer CHARLES H. LORING, U. S. N.
SIMEON B. CHITTENDEN, of New York.
WILLIAM H. WADSWORTH, of Kentucky.

EXTRACT FROM THE REGULATIONS OF THE NAVAL ACADEMY.

CHAP. VI, SEC. 9.—The Secretary of the Navy will, when expedient, annually invite not less than seven persons, such as he may judge well qualified, to attend at the academy during the May examina-tion as a Board of Visitors, for the purpose of witnessing the examination of the graduating and other classes, and of examining into the state of the police, discipline, and general management of the institu-tion; the result of which examination they will report to the Secretary of the Navy.

ACADEMIC BOARD.

DAVID D. PORTER, Vice-Admiral, *President.*

NAPOLEON B. HARRISON, Captain...... *Commandant of Midshipmen, Head of Department of Sea-manship, Gunnery, Naval and Infantry Tactics, &c.*

JOSEPH S. SKERRETT, Commander ..... *Assistant to Commandant of Midshipmen, in charge of De-partment of Seamanship, &c.*

EDWARD TERRY, Lieut. Com'r........... *Assistant to Commandant of Midshipmen, in charge of De-partment of Gunnery, &c.*

GEORGE DEWEY, Lieut. Com'r........... *Assistant to Commandant of Midshipmen, in Executive Duty in charge of Vessels.*

CHARLES L. FRANKLIN, Lieut. Com'r... *Assistant to Commandant of Midshipmen, in Executive Duty.*

WILLIAM H. WILLCOX, Professor....... *Head of Department of Mathematics.*

HENRY L. SNYDER, 1st Asst. Engineer .. *Head of Department of Steam Enginery.*

ROBERT L. PHYTHIAN, Lieut. Com'r .... *Head of Department of Astronomy, Navigation, &c.*

WILLIAM T. SAMPSON, Lieut. Com'r.... *Head of Department of Natural and Experimental Philos-ophy.*

THOMAS L. SWANN, Lieut. Com'r........ *Head of Department of Ethics and English Studies.*

OFFICERS OF THE NAVAL ACADEMY.

Vice-Admiral DAVID D. PORTER, *Superintendent.*
JAMES M. ALDEN, *Secretary to the Vice-Admiral.*

ACADEMIC STAFF.

Captain NAPOLEON B. HARRISON .... *Commandant of Midshipmen, Head of Department of Sea-manship, Gunnery, Naval and Infantry Tactics, &c.*

Commander JOSEPH S. SKERRETT......... *Assistant to Commandant of Midshipmen, and Senior Instructor in Seamanship, Naval Tactics, Naval Construction, &c.*

Lieut. Com'r SILAS CASEY ....
Lieut. Com'r JOHN F. McGLENSEY ......
Lieut. Com'r ERNEST J. DICHMAN......
Lieutenant THOMAS P. WILSON ....
Ass't Naval Constructor THEO. D. WILSON
} *Assistants to Commandant of Midshipmen, and Assistant Instructors in Seamanship, Naval Tactics, Naval Construction, &c.*

Lieut. Com'r EDWARD TERRY .... *Assistant to Commandant of Midshipmen, and Senior Instructor in Naval Gunnery, Infantry Tactics. and Howitzer Drill.*

Lieut. Com'r GEORGE W. HAYWARD ...
Lieut. Com'r CHARLES S. COTTON.......
Lieut. Com'r GEORGE W. COFFIN........
Lieut. Com'r GEORGE H. WADLEIGH. ..
} *Assistants to Commandant of Midshipmen and Assistant Instructors in Naval Gunnery, Infantry Tactics, and Howitzer Drill.*

Lieut. Com'r GEORGE DEWEY .... *Assistant to Commandant of Midshipmen, in charge of Practice Ships and other vessels.*

Lieut. Com'r CHARLES L. FRANKLIN ....*Assistant to Commandant of Midshipmen, and Senior Assistant in Executive Duty.*

Lieut. Com'r HENRY F. PICKING.........
Lieut. Com'r SILAS W. TERRY ....
Lieut. Com'r WILLIAM B. HOFF ....
Lieut. Com'r GEORGE D. B. GLIDDEN ...
} *Assistants to Commandant of Midshipmen, in Executive Duty.*

MATHEMATICS.

WILLIAM H. WILCOX, Professor........... *Head of Department of Mathematics.*
ALLAN D. BROWN, Lieut. Com'r ....
PURN'L F. HARRINGTON, Lieut. Com'r.
FRANCIS A. COOK, Lieut. Com'r ....
} *Assistant Instructors in Mathematics.*
JOHN M. RICE ....
WILLIAM W. JOHNSON....................
CHARLES F. JOHNSON....................
} *Assistant Professors of Mathematics.*

STEAM ENGINERY.

HENRY L. SNYDER, 1st Ass't Eng'r .... *Head of Department of Steam Enginery.*
CHARLES E. DeVALIN, 1st Ass't Eng'r ..
EDWARD B. LATCH, 1st Ass't Eng'r ....
GEORGE W. ROCHE, 2d Ass't Eng'r ......
JOHN C. KAFER, 2d Ass't Eng'r ....
ROBERT CRAWFORD, 2d Ass't Eng'r .....
} *Assistant Instructors in Steam Enginery.*

ASTRONOMY, ETC.

ROBERT L. PHYTHIAN, Lieut. Com'r ...... *Head of the Department of Astronomy, Navigation, and Surveying.*

JOHN A. HOWELL, Lieut. Com'r.......... } *Assistant Instructors in Astronomy, Navigation, and Surveying.*
LEWIS CLARK, Lieut. Com'r .... }

CHARLES J. WHITE .... *Assistant Professor of Astronomy, Navigation, and Surveying.*

NATURAL AND EXPERIMENTAL PHILOSOPHY.

WILLIAM T. SAMPSON, Lieut. Com'r ...... *Head of Department of Natural and Experimental Philosophy.*

RICHARD H. THURSTON, 1st Ass't Eng'r } *Assistant Instructors in Natural and Experimental Philosophy.*
JOHN PEMBERTON, 2d Ass't Eng'r ...... }

ETHICS, ETC.

THOMAS L. SWANN, Lieut. Com'r.......... *Head of Department of Ethics and English Studies.*
ARTHUR H. WRIGHT, Lieut. Com'r ......
EDWARD M. STEDMAN, Lieut. Com'r ...
CHARLES H. BLACK, Lieutenant......... } *Assistant Instructors in Ethics and English Studies.*
FRANCIS H. SHEPPARD, Master ....
THOMAS KARNEY..................... *Professor of Ethics and English Studies.*
WILLIAM W. FAY.....................
JOSEPH E. DICKSON .... } *Assistant Professors of Ethics and English Studies.*
JOHN J. ARCHER.....................

FRENCH.

LEOPOLD V. DOVILLIERS, Professor ...... *Head of Department of French.*
ALPHONSE V. S. COURCELLE ....
LUCIEN F. PRUD'HOMME ....
EUGENE DOVILLIERS .... } *Assistant Professors of French.*
JULES LEROUX.....................
BERNARD MAURICE ....

SPANISH.

EDWARD A. ROGET, Professor .... *Head of Department of Spanish.*
CHARLES F. BLAKE, Lieut. Com'r .... *Assistant Instructor in Spanish.*
PEDRO MONTALDO...................... } *Assistant Professors of Spanish.*
JAMES P. MARRON .... }

DRAWING.

AUGUSTUS P. COOKE, Lieut, Com'r .... *Head of Department of Drawing.*
CHARLES D. SIGSBEE, Lieut. Com'r........ *Assistant Instructor in Drawing.*
MARSHAL OLIVER .... } *Assistant Professors of Drawing.*
ANDREW W. WARREN .... }

NATURAL HISTORY, ETC.

HENRY H. LOCKWOOD, Professor.......... *Head of Department of Natural History and Mineralogy*

ART OF DEFENSE.

ANTOINE J. CORBESIER................... *Sword Master.*
THEODORE MAURICE................... } *Assistant Sword Masters.*
ADOLPHE AUBRY .... }
MATHEW STROHM .... *Boxing Master and Gymnast.*

OFFICERS NOT ATTACHED TO THE ACADEMIC STAFF.

Commander JAMES A. GREER, U. S. N.....*In charge of Grounds, &c.*
Captain McLANE TILTON, U. S. M. C ....*Commanding Marine Guard.*
1st Lieut. WILLIAM S. MUSE, U. S. M.C......*Assistant to Commanding Officer.*
2d Lieut. SAMUEL K. ALLEN, U. S. M.C......*Assistant to Commanding Officer.*
EDWARD SHIPPEN.....................*Surgeon.*

GEORGE H. COOKE ....*Passed Assistant Surgeon.*
LUTHER M. LYON ....*Passed Assistant Surgeon.*
CALVIN C. JACKSON........................*Paymaster.*
JAMES HOY, Jr.............................*Paymaster, (Storekeeper.)*
DONALD McLAREN ....*Chaplain.*
RICHARD SWANN ....*Commissary.*
JAMES J. GRAFF ....*Assistant Librarian.*
RICHARD M. CHASE........................*Secretary of the Academy.*
DAVID E. PORTER ....*First Clerk.*
OWEN D. ROBB.............................*Second Clerk.*
JAMES TILTON ....*Third Clerk.*

JAMES HUTCHINSON ....*Gunner.*
JOHN SOUTHWICK..........................*Carpenter.*

MIDSHIPMEN ON PROBATION AT THE NAVAL ACADEMY,

ARRANGED

IN ORDER OF MERIT IN THEIR RESPECTIVE CLASSES,

AS DETERMINED AT THE

GENERAL EXAMINATION IN MAY, 1869.

TOGETHER WITH

THE MIDSHIPMEN ADMITTED IN JUNE AND SEPTEMBER, 1869, FORMING
THE FOURTH CLASS OF 1869-70.

NOTES.

Midshipmen whose names are marked thus (*) are the five most distinguished in their respective classes.

Those marked thus (†) were found deficient, but were allowed to continue in their classes on condition of passing at a re-examination.

Those marked thus (‡) were found deficient, and turned back to recommence the studies of their respective classes.

Those marked thus (§) were found deficient, and recommended for discharge.

MIDSHIPMEN ON PROBATION AT THE NAVAL ACADEMY.

First Class—Graduating Class of 1869—78 Members.

Order of general merit.	NAME.	STATE.	DATE OF ADMISSION.	Age Years	Age Months	Seamanship	Naval tactics	Naval construction	Gunnery, &c.	Fencing	Steam enginery	Navigation	Physics	International law	French	Spanish	No. of demerits	Conduct	Sea service Months	Sea service Days
*1	Charles P. Perkins	Massachusetts	July 21, 1865	17	5	14	4	2	4	40	6	3	1	1	1	3	26	12	8	10
*2	Edwin H. Wiley	Ills.	July 28, 1865	17	10	2	2	21	1	37	18	11	2	2	19	20	24	9	8	10
*3	Henry M. M. Richards	Pennsylvania	July 21, 1865	16	11	47	60	3	12	55	16	7	7	12	7	7	10	5	8	10
*4	Sumner C. Paine	Maine	Sept. 22, 1865	17	11	5	0	1	15	63	8	9	12	7	37	28	96	57	8	10
*5	Benjamin H. Buckingham	Ohio	July 22, 1865	17	5	7	10	13	5	46	4	46	14	12	22	36	32	15	8	10
6	Louis E. Bixler	Pennsylvania	Sept. 27, 1865	16	8	23	3	18	27	7	2	13	4	24	27	24	0	1	8	10
7	William W. Kimball	Son of officer	July 31, 1865	16	7	4	20	16	3	14	3	49	20	2	39	27	26	12	8	10
8	Charles R. Brown	New Hampshire	Sept. 16, 1865	16	10	21	30	5	10	56	21	1	6	12	9	2	84	52	8	10
9	Giles B. Harber	Ohio	Sept. 22, 1865	16	7	9	36	10	33	4	8	5	6	33	4	4	62	36	8	10
10	Clinton K. uriis	West Virginia	July 22, 1865	16	10	6	8	17	38	17	12	14	13	49	43	29	48	26	8	10
11	William P. Baer	New York	Sept. 28, 1865	15	5	17	13	11	39	27	4	11	33	26	7	16	42	21	8	10
12	John B. H bs m.	Iowa	Sept. 27, 1865	15	4	10	6	33	8	43	8	4	5	2	12	8	74	41	8	10
13	John B. Briggs	Massachusetts	July 28, 1865	16	8	18	5	4	17	31	6	17	8	11	2	12	80	49	8	10
14	Charles G. Bowman	Indiana	Sept. 30, 1865	16	2	18	18	23	2	17	38	2	16	6	15	1	44	22	8	10
15	Baird A. Field	Connecticut	July 29, 1865	16	6	3	12	34	32	11	29	37	23	8	4	20	54	30	8	10
16	William H. Turner	Ohio	Sept. 22, 1865	17	9	26	16	14	34	65	39	22	26	9	45	39	0	1	8	10
17	Alexander M. Thackara	Pennsylvania	July 22, 1865	16	10	29	11	6	34	26	55	6	17	15	5	6	76	45	8	10
18	John Garvin	Ohio	July 21, 1865	16	6	11	38	25	7	28	30	11	15	33	36	41	34	16	8	10
19	John C. Wilson	New York	July 22, 1865	16	9	28	7	18	13	46	27	5	19	10	42	12	48	26	8	10
20	Fletcher S. Bassett	Illinois	July 24, 1865	17	4	21	44	9	14	51	5	8	3	24	14	15	120	62	8	10
21	Henry O. Handy	Massachusetts	July 25, 1865	14	9	1	24	32	16	69	12	72	54	55	66	53	44	26	8	10
22	Newton E. Mason	Pennsylvania	Sept. 21, 1865	17	11	24	1	20	6	37	33	10	11	67	65	25	48	22	8	10
23	Arthur P. Osborn	Ohio	July 24, 1865	15	10	9	13	10	17	31	22	27	22	20	56	29	44	24	8	10
24	Uriah R. Harris	Indiana	July 31, 1865	16	10	39	6	61	24	21	22	33	49	2	22	60	70	40	8	10
25	Herbert Winslow	Son of officer	July 22, 1865	16	10	44	30	7	20	56	18	21	38	39	6	10	0	1	8	10
26	Edward J. Berwind	Pennsylvania	July 21, 1865	16	10	64	4	43	30	29	34	39	21	4	9	48	90	54	8	10
27	Kossuth Niles	Wis.	July 21, 1865	15	1	40	28	38	37	31	16	22	65	47	53	9	24	9	8	10
28	Frank C. Day	Son of officer	Sept. 23, 1865	16	3	11	74	24	9	31	16	19	24	55	48	13	60	34	8	10
29	Elliott J. Arthur	Ills.	July 25, 1865	15	8	33	17	21	45	23	30	30	32	19	29	42	36	17	8	10
30	Nathaniel J. K. Patch	Massachusetts	Sept. 27, 1865	17	5	58	57	58	21	70	33	37	44	26	34	54	46	24	8	10
31	Karl Rohrer	Missouri	Sept. 21, 1865	17	4	46	69	34	25	41	1	35	39	19	34	26	0	1	8	10
32	William E. B. Delahay	Kansas	July 22, 1865	17	4	43	23	34	25	71	1	48	39	26	34	22	78	48	11	5

No.	Name	State / Remarks	Date	Year
33	James Franklin	Maryland	Sept. 26,	1865
34	John A. Norris	Pennsylvania	Sept. 28,	1865
35	John Milligan	Ohio	July 21,	1865
36	Richard G. Davenport	Georgia	Sept. 29,	1864
37	William P. Day	Naval apprentice	July 26,	1865
38	Charles W. Ruschenberger	Son of officer	July 23,	1864
39	Timothy D. Bolles	Mass.	Oct. 1,	1864
40	William F. Bulkley	New York	July 20,	1865
41	Charles A. Bradbury	Vermont	July 27,	1865
42	Geo. P. Colvocoresses	Son of officer	Sept. 28,	1864
43	Charles A. Clarke	Iowa	July 21,	1864
44	John A. H. Nickels	Mississippi	Oct. 8,	1864
45	Arthur P. Nazro	Massachusetts	July 22,	1865
46	Dennis Mahan	Son of officer	July 21,	1865
47	Geo. F. Wright	Illinois	July 21,	1865
48	Edward B. Barry	Son of officer	July 21,	1865
49	William H. Driggs	Michigan	July 21,	1865
50	Frederick B. Hull	Michigan	Sept. 30,	1865
51	John H. Moore	New York	July 31,	1865
52	Samuel P. Comly	New Jersey	July 21,	1865
53	Daniel D. V. Stuart	New York	Sept. 23,	1863
54	Nelson T. Houston	New York	July 21,	1865
55	Horace A. ...hard	Massachusetts	Sept. 26,	1865
56	Richard A. Breck	Massachusetts	Sept. 30,	1865
57	William C. Negley	Pennsylvania	Sept. 26,	1865
58	Edward O. Macfarlane	Pennsylvania	July 3,	1864
59	Wainwright Kellogg	Pennsylvania	Sept. 24,	1865
60	Emory H. Taunt	Pennsylvania	July 24,	1865
61	John H. C. Coffin	Son of officer	July 26,	1864
62	John P. Wallis	Maryland	July 30,	1864
63	Henry C. Longnecker	Pennsylvania	July 30,	1865
64	Henry T. Monahon	Naval apprentice	July 26,	1865
65	Thomas S. Phelps	Son of officer	July 26,	1865
66	Charles E. Colahan	Pennsylvania	July 21,	1865
67	William A. Hadden	Pennsylvania	Sept. 28,	1865
68	James W. Graydon	Indiana	July 22,	1865
69	Henry T. Stockton	Pennsylvania	July 22,	1865
70	Albert G. Berry	At large	July 25,	1865
71	Giles Seymour	Oregon	Sept. 28,	1864
72	William F. Low	New Hampshire	July 24,	1865
73	Sidney H. May	New Hampshire	July 28,	1864
74	Richard Mitchell	Massachusetts	July 22,	1864
75	Martin E. Hall	Iowa	Sept. 19,	1865
76	Alfred B. Fowler	Naval apprentice	Sept. 23,	1865
77	William S. King	Dakota Territory	July 31,	1865
78	George A. Zabriskie	Nebraska Territory	Sept. 29,	1865

Second Class—70 Members—1869.

Order of general merit	NAME	STATE	DATE OF ADMISSION	Age Yrs	Age Mos	Seamanship	Gunnery, &c.	Infantry tactics	Fencing	Mathematics	Steam enginery	Astronomy and navigation	Mechanics	French	Spanish	Number of demerits	Conduct	Sea service Mos	Sea service Days
*1	George L. Dyer	Maine	July 26, 1866	16	10	3	6	9	15	5	1	8	4	2	1	8	1	9	10
*2	Hawley O. Rittenhouse	New Jersey	July 27, 1866	15	1	8	10	7	24	1	7	2	1	14	7	58	17	9	10
*3	Winfield S. Baker	Indiana	July 30, 1866	17	5	11	4	10	3	2	5	12	2	24	30	44	9	9	10
*4	Henry W. Schaefer	Illinois	July 23, 1866	16	5	32	4	8	34	4	10	6	9	12	6	18	3	9	10
*5	Robert G. Peck	Massachusetts	Sept. 24, 1866	17	2	19	1	0	23	7	9	3	2	5	2	40	7	9	10
6	Charles Briggs	Rhode Island	July 30, 1866	17	4	16	8	10	29	6	10	1	1	16	21	40	7	9	10
7	Herman F. Fickbohm	Naval apprentice	July 31, 1866	17	2	21	3	5	28	9	16	7	10	26	10	82	28	8	10
8	John Hubbard	Arizona Territory	July 26, 1866	16	9	2	11	4	56	16	33	13	5	21	3	68	5	9	10
9	Alexander McCrackin	Iowa	July 27, 1866	16	0	14	20	6	9	12	8	16	11	35	14	172	21	9	10
10	William G. Mayer	Ohio	July 31, 1866	16	11	23	6	23	60	11	33	10	7	8	4	68	23	9	10
11	Henry Harris	Illinois	Aug. 1, 1866	16	7	35	2	3	16	8	2	8	1	34	18	48	58	9	10
12	John W. Danenhower	Illinois	Sept. 25, 1866	17	1	29	8	15	34	15	20	5	5	28	20	48	11	9	10
13	Lewis C. Heilner	Pennsylvania	July 25, 1866	16	10	18	21	17	30	3	36	11	6	46	25	38	11	9	10
14	Samuel L. Graham	Pennsylvania	July 27, 1866	17	6	24	21	17	62	21	20	14	19	17	15	120	6	9	10
15	Joel A. Post	New York	July 26, 1866	15	5	12	18	23	10	20	24	18	9	1	8	48	32	9	10
16	Joseph B. Murdock	Massachusetts	July 23, 1866	15	7	28	25	21	70	23	28	4	14	29	12	38	43	9	10
17	John D. Keeler	Indiana	July 25, 1866	17	5	9	9	26	48	29	41	15	31	27	13	86	26	9	10
18	Lazarus L. Reamey	Pennsylvania	July 31, 1866	17	0	20	13	10	41	50	54	17	11	23	57	75	2	9	10
19	George A. Calhoun	Naval apprentice	July 27, 1866	17	0	13	12	1	50	30	12	31	26	50	43	12	4	9	10
20	Walter S. Holliday	Wisconsin	July 31, 1866	16	2	5	27	40	57	18	26	20	13	45	24	20	35	8	10
21	Charles P. Kunhardt	Pennsylvania	July 31, 1866	15	11	26	18	19	1	17	3	23	27	3	16	98	55	9	10
22	Harry M. Jacoby	Pennsylvania	July 27, 1866	17	11	33	41	56	34	14	16	39	47	31	17	148	15	9	10
23	Corwin P. Rees	Ohio	July 30, 1866	16	10	46	49	52	60	28	41	45	16	30	23	52	25	9	10
24	Jacob J. Hunker	Ohio	July 23, 1866	16	9	14	35	15	19	25	63	44	31	36	46	74	14	9	10
25	Nathan Sargent	Montana Territory	Sept. 27, 1866	17	8	27	33	29	44	33	13	21	21	4	21	216	67	9	10
26	Whitmul P. Ray	Indiana	July 31, 1866	16	9	53	17	2	49	46	41	44	38	49	62	142	51	9	10
27	Landon P. Jouett	Kentucky	July 24, 1866	16	6	22	38	26	21	33	14	21	24	47	18	132	48	9	10
28	Greenlief A. Merriam	Massachusetts	July 24, 1866	16	8	44	29	59	21	46	14	19	30	59	53	46	10	9	10

No.	Name	State	Date
29	Haile C. Nye	Ohio	July 28, 1866
30	William M. Wood	Indiana	July 24, 1865
31	Miers F. Wright	Pennsylvania	Oct. 1, 1865
32	James L. Carter	New York	July 25, 1866
33	Edward M. Hughes	At large	July 26, 1866
34	Charles E. Vreeland	Iowa	July 31, 1866
35	Clayton S. Richman	Naval apprentice	July 24, 1866
36	Marcus D. Hyde	Washington Territory	Nov. 25, 1865
37	William P. Conway	Kentucky	Oct. 1, 1866
38	Boynton Leach	New York	July 30, 1866
39	George W. Holman	California	July 25, 1866
40	Thomas C. Spencer	Son of officer	July 25, 1866
41	John S. Abbot	Wisconsin	Sept. 23, 1864
42	Charles H. Lyman	Ohio	July 26, 1866
43	John B. Collins	Louisiana	July 30, 1866
44	William Remsen	New York	July 26, 1866
45	Henry R. Penington	Delaware	Oct. 1, 1866
46	Charles F. Emmerich	District of Columbia	Sept. 26, 1866
47	Why G. C. Salter	Naval apprentice	Sept. 24, 1866
48	John P. J. At	Son of officer	Sept. 26, 1866
49	James H. Bull	Pennsylvania	July 25, 1866
50	William H. Van de Carr	New York	July 24, 1865
51	Martial C. Dimock	Naval apprentice	July 31, 1866
52	Hugo Osterhaus	Missouri	Sept. 22, 1865
53	Freeman H. Crosby	New York	July 30, 1866
54	Wie Kilburn	California	Dec. 5, 1865
55	Ferdinand H.	Ohio	July 22, 1865
56	Anson B.	Naval apprentice	July 31, 1866
57	John B. Milton	Kentucky	July 30, 1866
58	Hanson R. Tyler	Vermont	July 27, 1866
59	James H. Sawyers	Kentucky	Sept. 24, 1866
60	Joseph H.	Illinois	Sept. 22, 1865
61	Francis L. Ludlow	New	July 24, 1866
62	Albert C. Dillingham	Pennsylvania	July 21, 1865
63	James M. Gore	Son of officer	July 25, 1866
64		Ohio	July 26, 1866
65	George W. Mentz	New Jersey	Sept. 26, 1866
66	Theodoric Porter	Son of officer	Sept. 23, 1866
67	Henry L. Green	New York	July 31, 1866
68	Frank Ellery, jr.	Son of officer	Sept. 25, 1866
69	Francis Winslow	Son of officer	July 22, 1866
++	James P. Norton	Connecticut	July 26, 1866

Third Class—55 Members—1869.

Order of general merit	NAME	STATE	DATE OF ADMISSION	Age Years	Age Months	Seamanship	Gunnery, &c.	Fencing	Mathematics	Chemistry	History and composition	Rhetoric	French	Spanish	Drawing	Number of demerits	Conduct	Sea service Months	Sea service Days
*1	Sidney A. Stanton	West. Va.	Sept. 20, 1867	17	0	2	1	8	1	1	3	1	9	5	18	28	4	6	3
*2	Charles Terrill	Kentucky	Sept. 25, 1867	16	0	3	4	33	2	3	8	5	7	6	4	16	1	6	3
*3	Aaron Ward	Pennsylvania	Sept. 26, 1867	15	11	6	2	1	3	2	2	3	1	1	27	46	11	6	3
*4	Chauncey Thomas	Pennsylvania	Sept. 25, 1867	15	4	4	5	10	12	12	9	9	28	24	5	24	3	6	3
*5	Charles W. Bartlett	Massachusetts	June 20, 1867	16	10	14	6	3	5	14	15	12	36	37	9	42	8	6	3
6	William M. Irwin	Ohio	Sept. 28, 1867	17	7	23	13	9	6	7	1	2	18	11	26	54	16	6	3
7	Perrin Busbee	At large	Sept. 30, 1867	17	7	9	10	25	7	17	6	4	16	17	39	94	25	6	3
8	Frank W. Nabor	Mo.	Sept. 20, 1867	17	7	26	22	14	8	16	22	18	30	27	11	28	4	6	3
9	Benjamin C. Tillinghast	Naval apprentice	July 31, 1866	17	5	5	8	16	18	9	12	11	19	22	10	134	37	6	10
10	Carlos G. Calkins	Ohio	Sept. 20, 1867	16	3	13	7	42	9	28	5	1	11	16	49	62	17	9	10
11	William P. Clason	Rhode Island	June 20, 1867	17	9	22	15	7	27	5	7	6	2	20	3	110	30	6	3
12	Henry H. Barroll	Missouri	Sept. 27, 1866	16	4	31	35	33	13	11	13	24	33	13	15	160	33	9	3
13	Albert A. Crandall	Minnesota	Sept. 27, 1867	17	3	15	13	2	25	6	4	9	17	8	40	94	8	6	3
14	Albert J. Dabney	Kentucky	June 29, 1867	17	7	10	3	48	22	24	11	7	39	21	50	112	22	6	3
15	Julius C. Freeman	Illinois	Sept. 23, 1867	17	3	25	23	5	19	18	41	8	43	34	7	42	13	6	10
16	Thos. C. Hanus	Wisconsin	Oct. 4, 1866	17	6	36	32	40	11	39	26	16	3	7	16	88	33	12	4
17	Walter S. French	Maine	July 26, 1865	14	4	38	37	40	17	12	19	32	4	4	20	48	46	9	10
18	Thos. C. Cresap	Ohio	July 27, 1866	17	8	46	44	54	4	24	42	22	36	17	13	112	44	6	3
19	William H. E. Masser	Pennsylvania	June 22, 1867	17	9	11	16	44	10	18	16	20	46	15	1	168	20	9	3
20	John E. Roller	Naval apprentice	Oct. 1, 1866	15	3	12	11	51	43	39	49	51	25	13	19	74	53	6	10
21	Joseph H. Fraunces	Pennsylvania	June 20, 1867	16	10	17	26	12	15	20	16	26	15	10	17	204	43	6	3
22	Joseph L. Hunsicker	Pennsylvania	July 26, 1866	16	5	8	28	25	20	20	36	31	15	14	44	152	36	6	3
23	Ben. B. Scott	Iowa	July 24, 1867	15	2	34	36	25	29	29	4	15	23	13	51	126	48	6	3
24	William P. Elliott	At large	June 28, 1867	16	7	24	42	24	14	4	27	13	14	17	42	186	35	6	3
25	Horace P. McIntosh	Indiana	Sept. 25, 1867	15	4	7	10	10	21	43	21	13	19	38	33	120	24	6	3
26	Thomas C. Wood	New York	June 27, 1867	16	5	16	24	17	28	37	28	11	28	43	32	92	11	9	3
27	Frederick H. Lefavor	Ohio	July 30, 1866	17	2	29	12	13	37	38	34	25	52	35	8	46	10	9	10
28	John Downes†	At large	June 20, 1867	15	7	19	—	—	34	55d	37	36	19	—	32	44	—	6	3

No.	Name	State	Date			
29	Downes L. Won	At large	July 27, 1866			
30	Edward F. Qualtrough	New York	Sept. 20, 1867			
31	Henry L. Selden	Connecticut	July 27, 1866			
32	Francis E. Greene	Indiana	July 24, 1866			
33	Henry Ola	Indiana	Sept. 24, 1867			
34	Hias S. Plunket	At large	June 20, 1867			
35	Robert D. Stevens	New York	June 27, 1867			
36	Alphonzo H.	Michigan	Sept. 21, 1867			
37	James M. Wight	Michigan	June 29, 1867			
38	Frank Guertin	Wisconsin	June 28, 1867			
39	Christopher Bruns	New York	June 28, 1867			
40	Charles A. Foster	Massachusetts	Aug. 1, 1866			
41	Frank B. Veazie	Massachusetts	July 23, 1866			
42	William A. Marshall	Pennsylvania	June 26, 1867			
43	Charles D. Galloway	Maryland	Sept. 22, 1866			
44	Wm E. Sewell	New York	Sept. 25, 1867			
45	William H. Slack	At large	Sept. 28, 1867			
46	Asher C. Baker	Iowa	Sept. 25, 1867			
47	George A. Sanderson	Ohio	Sept. 26, 1866			
48	Whipple	Son of officer	Sept. 25, 1866			
49	Wm C. Babcock	Kansas	Sept. 23, 1867			
50	John T. Edson	At large	June 25, 1867			
51	Frank S.	New York	June 27, 1867			
52	Jeremiah C. Burnett	Indiana	Sept. 20, 1867			
53	Geo A. Vail	New York	Sept. 26, 1867			

Fourth Class—50 Members—1869.

Order of general merit.	NAME.	STATE.	DATE OF ADMISSION.	Age at date of admission. Years.	Age at date of admission. Months.	ORDER OF MERIT IN— Seamanship.	Mathematics.	Grammar.	Geography.	History and composition.	Drawing.	Number of demerits.	Conduct.	Sea service in practice ships. Months.	Days.
*1	... C. Smith	New ...	June 27, 1868	17	5	6	5	3	5	5	1	12	3	1	13
*2	Albert T. Freeman	New Jersey	Sept. 24, 1868	17	11	21	4	2	7	2	5	27	5	3	13
*3	William H. H. Sutherland	Naval apprentice	June 22, 1868	15	1	10	6	7	1	1	9	265	44	3	28
*4	Jesse M. Roper	Missouri	June 24, 1868	16	7	7	2	6	12	4	46	8	1	3	28
*5	... A. Thompson	Louisiana	Sept. 23, 1868	17	1	31	8	5	2	8	11	48	8	3	13
6	Charles E. Fox	At large	June 23, 1868	16	9	19	15	8	11	6	2	34	7	3	28
7	George T. Winst...	North Carolina	Sept. 30, 1868	15	11	35	1	1	20	2	37	87	2	3	13
8	Ja... Medary	At large	Sept. 25, 1868	15	7	9	13	1	2	23	2	54	10	4	28
9	Joel A. Barber	Wisconsin	June 20, 1867	17	4	24	3	4	10	11	6	221	38	3	27
10	Robert H. ...	At large	June 24, 1868	16	1	12	12	24	34	14	3	113	26	3	28
11	Milton K. Schwenk	Colorado Territory	Sept. 22, 1866	16	4	10	9	22	14	28	10	67	16	3	13
12	Frank H. Powers	Naval apprentice	June 22, 1868	15	0	2	10	20	9	16	12	59	12	3	28
13	Rob... S. Graham	New Jers...	Sept. 20, 1867	14	11	29	28	12	8	21	47	78	20	3	13
14	Samuel Seabury, (R)	Naval apprentice	June 20, 1867	17	6	13	33	19	16	9	13	48	8	3	28
15	Howard S. Waring	Naval apprentice	Sept. 26, 1867	17	5	30	31	9	3	6	4	163	35	3	13
16	Germaine B. Vandervoort	Naval apprentice	June 22, 1867	17	3	5	16	17	24	11	43	235	39	3	28
17	Robert H. McLean	Naval apprentice	June 27, 1868	16	7	23	18	21	2	21	30	241	40	3	28
18	Charl... R. Miles	Utah Territory	June 20, 1868	16	8	4	17	29	28	9	38	69	18	3	13
19	Frederick Tyler	Michigan	June 23, 1868	16	1	20	24	15	24	15	39	279	45	3	28
20	Oswin W. Lowry	Ohio	Sept. 24, 1868	16	4	15	27	25	18	32	7	20	4	2	28
21	... H. Garrett	Tennessee	Sept. 23, 1868	17	3	16	25	29	5	27	8	60	13	3	13
22	Benjamin F. Rinehart	Pennsylvania	Sept. 25, 1868	17	8	42	29	25	15	26	31	10	6	3	28
23	Daniel F. Bak...	At large	June 20, 1868	14	6	42	23	29	40	38	27	31	27	3	28
24	Rogers H. ...	Wisconsin	June 26, 1867	16	10	18	7	13	25	35	29	126	24	3	13
25	... ...	At large	June 22, 1868	17	3	2	19	16	19	17	22	106	30	2	28
26	Jon. G. Dietrich	Illinois	Sept. 22, 1868	17	9	1	36	10	23	20	17	153	30	2	13
27	Frank E. Sawyer	Massachusetts	Sept. 20, 1867	16	9	24	32	39	43	31	21	213	36	2	13

	Name	State	Date														
28	John C. ____, jr	At large	June 24, 1868	17	2	14	31	29	26	28	20	164	3	34	3	28
29	Fred V. Dockery	North Carolina	Sept. 23, 1868	17	6	37	34	37	12	17	24	87	2	22	1	13
30	Wm C. Heacock	New York	Sept. 22, 1868	17	6	36	26	36	16	35	45	110	3	25	3	13
31	John H. Leyth	West Va.	June 25, 1868	17	2	28	20	43	32	35	23	130	3	28	2	28
32	William Polmyer	At large	June 20, 1868	14	6	33	37	27	38	40	26	60	3	13	3	13
33	Oren P. Lasher	New York	Sept. 26, 1868	17	11	39	14	27	22	16	49	262	2	43	2	13
34	James H. Winlock †	Kentucky	Sept. 21, 1868	16	5	26	27	44	37	30	28	67	3	16	2	28
35	Nathaniel T. James	At large	June 27, 1868	15	11	8	35	35	29	36	44	248	2	41	3	13
36	Geo W. Hey	New York	S pta 29, 1868	16	6	47	33	38	42	23	36	57	3	11	2	13
37	Vincendon L. Cottman	New York	S pta 21, 1868	16	7	48	33	33	41	16	34	79	2	31	3	13
38	Charles H. Crosswait	Indiana	June 24, 1868	16	8	30	29	29	30	34	25	156	3	31	2	28
39	Charles T. Mitchell	Tennessee	Sept. 25, 1868	14	2	45	42	30	41	25	42	150	2	33	3	13
	William M. Slough	New Mexico Territory	Sept. 26, 1868	14	1	41	def.	39	39	42	40	431	2	def.	2	13
	John Y. Orr	Arkansas	Sept. 26, 1868	16	9	49	def.	39	def.	49	48	489	2	def.	2	13
	Silas F. Dixen	Naval apprentice	Sept. 21, 1868	16	3	50	def.	34	def.	48	19	219	1	37	2	28
	Delmar R. Keeler	At large	June 22, 1868	17	8	46	def.	27	14	34	33	63	3	15	1	15
	William L. Pitcher	New York	June 29, 1868	17	6	3	23	14	48	19	15	77	1	19	0	13
	Ten Eyck De Witt Veeder	New York	Sept. 24, 1868	14	33	def.	48	36	37	44	304	2	47	0	14
	Alexander Kirkland	Maryland	Sept. 26, 1868	17	5	40	def.	45	45	50	429	def.	0	14
	Walter T. Livingston	Naval apprentice	June 20, 1867	17	11	41	def.	46	46	33	35	260	2	42	0	00
	James S. Manley	Maine	Sept. 29, 1868	14	5	37	def.	41	31	def.	18	158	2	32	0	00
	Rob K. Nagle	Naval apprentice	S pta 22, 1868	17	8	17	def.	39	43	def.	32	287	0	46	0	00
	Lemuel Van Epps	Naval apprentice	June 22, 1868	16	10	27	def.	46	47	def.	41	146	1	29	1	15

2 N A

(R) Re-examined in the studies of the Third Class, and ____ to it.

SUMMARY.

Academic Year 1868 and 1869 concluded June 4, 1869.

First, or Graduating Class	78 members.
Second Class	70 members.
Third Class	85 members.
Fourth Class	50 members.
Total	253

Alphabetical list of Midshipmen, eighty-seven (87) in number, admitted in June and September, forming the fourth class of 1869–'70.

Name.	State.	Date of admission.	Age at date of admission. Years.	Months.
John E. Anderson	Ohio	Sept. 22, 1869	17	5
George S. Arnold	South Carolina	June 29, 1869	17	9
Clinton J. Axson	Louisiana	June 24, 1869	16	4
Charles J. Badger	At large	June 22, 1869	15	10
Edward L. Baker	Iowa	Sept. 20, 1869	15	0
John W. Bean	North Carolina	June 23, 1869	16	0
James W. Blakely	Nevada	June 28, 1869	15	0
Charles J. Brenner	Missouri	Sept. 21, 1869	16	0
Richard W. Burns	Kentucky	June 22, 1869	16	2
Humberston S. Cannell	Georgia	Sept. 23, 1869	17	1
Augustus L. Case	At large	June 23, 1869	15	5
William N. Conet	Illinois	June 28, 1869	17	5
William H. Craig	Missouri	June 29, 1869	17	9
Walter C. Cowles	Connecticut	Sept. 21, 1869	16	2
Eben B. Crocker	Massachusetts	Sept. 22, 1869	15	4
Isaac B. Culp	Ohio	Sept. 22, 1869	16	5
Francis W. Danner	Alabama	June 23, 1869	17	7
Lewis J. Davids	New York	Sept. 22, 1869	15	0
Charles W. Deering	Maine	June 21, 1869	16	10
Jenness K. Dexter	At large	June 22, 1869	16	10
Samuel W. D. Diehl	Pennsylvania	Sept. 20, 1869	18	0
Isaac B. Elliot	South Carolina	Sept. 21, 1869	17	7
Harrison C. Fales	New York	June 29, 1869	15	7
John Farnsworth	Illinois	Sept. 25, 1869	14	0
Frank A. Fenn	Idaho Territory	June 22, 1869	15	9
Irving R. Fisher	Illinois	Sept. 23, 1869	16	10
Clarence E. Fithian	Ohio	Sept. 22, 1869	17	1
Gilbert Fowler	Massachusetts	June 23, 1869	15	1
Charles V. Grant	Tennessee	Sept. 23, 1869	14	11
Horatio W. Greenough	New York	June 24, 1869	15	9
William Gundlach	Illinois	Sept. 28, 1869	16	11
Richard Habersham	Georgia	Sept. 23, 1869	14	0
William F. Halsey	Louisiana	Sept. 21, 1869	16	5
Edwin F. Hard	New York	Sept. 22, 1869	16	4
Charles F. Holder	At large	June 23, 1869	16	10
Thomas B. Howard	At large	June 24, 1869	14	10
George W. Hyde	Maryland	Sept. 21, 1869	16	4
Jones M. Jackson	At large	Sept. 27, 1869	16	1
Frank T. Jenkins	At large	June 21, 1869	16	7
John P. Johnson	Georgia	June 21, 1869	16	1
James S. Jouett	At large	June 21, 1869	15	8
Austin M. Knight	Florida	June 30, 1869	14	6
Charles Laird	Ohio	Sept. 24, 1869	14	7
Samuel C. Lemly	North Carolina	June 26, 1869	16	3
James S. Manley	Maine	June 24, 1869	15	2
Charles M. McCartney	Pennsylvania	Sept. 23, 1869	15	1
William McKeloy	Pennsylvania	Sept. 24, 1869	16	10
Albert A. Michelson	At large	June 28, 1869	16	6
Frank J. Milligan	Tennessee	June 29, 1869	16	6
Charles B. T. Moore	Illinois	Sept. 27, 1869	16	1
Henry Morrell	New York	June 29, 1869	15	10
Thomas E. Muse	Maryland	Sept. 30, 1869	17	0
James S. Negley	Pennsylvania	Sept. 28, 1869	15	6
John B. Nichols	New York	Sept. 28, 1869	14	4
John O. Nicholson	Alabama	June 29, 1869	16	4
Reginald F. Nicholson	North Carolina	Sept. 30, 1869	16	9
George D. North	Tennessee	June 23, 1869	15	9
William A. Northcott	West Virginia	Sept. 24, 1869	15	7
David Peacock	New Jersey	Sept. 28, 1869	15	4
Herbert C. Pell	New York	June 28, 1869	16	5
Frank Pierson	New York	Sept. 22, 1869	16	6
Charles F. Putnam	Illinois	June 22, 1869	14	6
Eugene Raines	New York	June 23, 1869	17	2
Edmund G. Ray	Pennsylvania	Sept. 22, 1869	15	9
Alfred Reynolds	Indiana	Sept. 21, 1869	16	0
John F. Robb	Illinois	Sept. 22, 1869	16	5
John M. Robinson	At large	June 23, 1869	17	7
Hermann J. Rodman	Missouri	June 21, 1869	15	9
William H. Schuetze	Missouri	June 21, 1869	15	11
William F. Shaw	New Hampshire	Sept. 22, 1869	16	11
Mason A. Shufeldt	Connecticut	June 23, 1869	16	7
Irving Smith	Arkansas	June 24, 1869	17	9
Roaldo D. Strong	Ohio	June 26, 1869	16	2
William A. Talbott	Pennsylvania	Sept. 28, 1869	17	7
William V. B. Topping	Ohio	June 23, 1869	16	11
John W. Turnbull	At large	Oct. 5, 1869	17	4

Alphabetical list of Midshipmen, &c.—Continued.

Name.	State.	Date of admission.	Age at date of admission.	
			Years.	Months.
Edmund B. Underwood	At large	June 24, 1869	16	3
James P. Underwood	Michigan	June 28, 1869	17	7
Custis P. Upshur	South Carolina	Sept. 23, 1869	17	1
Edward Vail	Indiana	Sept. 21, 1869	15	10
Frederick C. C. Van Vliet	At large	June 21, 1869	15	6
Charles A. Wallingford	Indiana	Sept. 23, 1869	15	7
George B. Way	Maryland	Sept. 28, 1869	14	10
Frank A. White	Maine	Sept. 22, 1869	17	5
Frank A. Wilner	New York	June 29, 1869	17	10
William Winder	New Hampshire	Sept. 16, 1869	18	0
Lucien Young	Kentucky	June 21, 1869	17	2

SUMMARY.

Academic Year 1869–'70 begun October 1, 1869.

First Class .... 67 members..
Second Class .... 56 members.
Third Class.. 38 members.
Fourth Class, (appointments of 1869, and transfers from 1868)........... 92 members.

Total 253

CALENDAR—1869-'70.

1896.

June 21.— Examination of candidates for admission began............	Monday.
June 30.—Examination of candidates concluded.........................	Wednesday
July 4.—Holiday...	Sunday.
July 5.—The fourth observed; duties suspended.......................	Monday.
Sept. 20.—Examination of candidates for admission began............	Monday.
Sept. 30.—Examination of candidates concluded........................	Thursday.
Oct. 1.—Winter term began...	Friday.
Nov. 18.—Thanksgiving; studies and exercises suspended.............	Thursday.
Dec. 25.—Christmas; studies and exercises suspended..................	Saturday.
1870.	
Jan. 1.—New Year; studies and exercises suspended....................	Saturday.
Jan. 15.—Semi-annual examination begins.............................	Saturday.
Feb. 15.—Semi-annual examination and winter term ends..............	Tuesday.
Feb. 16.—Summer term begins...	Wednesday
Feb. 22.—Studies and exercises suspended.............................	Tuesday.
May 20.—Annual examination begins....................................	Friday.
June 10.—Annual examination and summer term ends.-.................	Friday.

PRACTICE CRUISE—1870.

1870-'71.

June 20.—Examination of candidates for admission begins............	Monday.
June 30.—Examination of candidates for admission ends..............	Thursday.
Sept. 20.—Examination of candidates for admission begins............	Tuesday.
Sept. 30.—Examination of candidates for admission ends..............	Friday.
Oct. 1.—Winter term begins...	Saturday.

COURSE OF INSTRUCTION.

The studies which shall be pursued and the instruction which shall be given at the Naval Academy are comprised under the following departments and branches :

FIRST DEPARTMENT—PRACTICAL SEAMANSHIP, NAVAL GUNNERY, AND NAVAL AND INFANTRY TACTICS.

First branch—Practical seamanship.—Mode of constructing, docking, and undocking vessels, and of heaving them down for examination and repair; preparations for, and stowage of, ballast, water, provisions, ammunition, sails, and other stores; getting on board and fitting in place masts, yards, rigging, sails, armament, boats, and all other articles of equipment, and arrangements for removing the same when a ship is to be dismantled; berthing the crew, and stationing the ship's company for various duties in working ship; unmooring ship; getting under way; anchoring and mooring; mode of using springs in the different cases to which they may be advantageously applied; keeping a ship from fouling her anchor; clearing hawse; practical use of the lead and of the helm; steering, tacking, wearing; making and shortening sail in different kinds of weather, and in different situations; backing and filling in a tideway; warping; heaving to and preserving relative position with other vessels when lying-to; chasing to windward and to leeward; closing with other vessels soonest, or avoiding them for the greatest length of time; towing one or more vessels, under all circumstances of weather, when towing is practicable; management of vessels and boats to save men who have fallen overboard, or to rescue persons from vessels at sea, when the sea is rough and dangerous; boarding vessels at sea; examination of ship's papers; landing in a heavy surf; watering and provisioning from an open beach; management of a vessel on her beam ends; also, when one or more masts are lost in a gale or in action; and when rudder is lost, or in danger from leaks in a gale at sea, or in imminent danger of soon foundering, or on fire at sea or in port; rules for avoiding collisions; rules of the road, and lights to be carried by vessels, as established by act of Congress.

Second branch—Theory and practice of gunnery—Practical naval gunnery.—The nomenclature of different parts of ships' guns, and of the different carriages which are used in the navy; and also the several uses, and the names of all articles belonging to or used with guns and carriages in action; component parts of gunpowder and mode of manufacture, and different means by which its strength and other qualities are or may be ascertained; mode of inspecting and proving guns, shot, and shells, for their reception from the makers; windage; manner of loading, fusing, and boxing shells, and of unloading them; testing quality and regulating length of fuses; arrangement of ship's magazines, shell, and shot rooms; dimensions of cartridge-bags, and mode of making them; weight of charges of powder for different calibers and distances; manner of fitting and using locks and tangent and dispart sights; necessity for guarding powder, shells, fuses, and all articles of which gunpowder forms a part, from moisture as well as from fire; preparation of a ship for action; stations and duties of men at guns of different calibers, in the different divisions, when preparing for quarters or action; exercise of the guns, and all the duties of those stationed at them in action; modes of ascertaining distances from vessels and other objects at sea; advantages of direct and of ricochet firing under different circumstances; ranges of different projectiles from different calibers and classes of guns; different modes of taking guns on board and sending them from vessels; of mounting and dismounting and transporting them; shifting carriages, breechings, and trucks; securing guns in heavy gales; managing and securing a gun that has got loose from breeching and tackles; means of gaining greater safe elevation and depression than carriages ordinarily afford; injurious effects of double shotting upon the recoil and safety of the gun, and upon the projectiles, as to the accuracy of their direction, and the extent of their range for penetration; arrangements for boarding and repelling boarders; different calls and signals used in action.

Furthermore, the use of boat and field guns; their nomenclature, weight, calibers, character, and construction, including the carriages with which they are used for boat and shore service; preparation of boats for their use; exercise when used in boats and when on shore; embarking them in boats from vessels; equipment for service against merchantmen, boats, or for shore service; mode of landing and embarking from the shore; construction and preparation, for immediate use, of the shrapnel and other shells, and of grape, and the regulation of the length of fuses; adaptation of the different kinds of projectile for service, according to distance, cover, and the character of the objects of attack; returning armament and equipments to the vessel, and disposition to be made of them on so doing.

Theory of gunnery.—Review of laws of motion, of projectiles in vacuo and in the atmosphere; initial, remaining, and final velocities, and the methods of determining their values; the effects on them by variations of charge, windage, and weight of projectiles; forces of deviation, arising from the motion of rotation and eccentricity of projectiles, from inclination of the axis of the trunnions, and from other causes; examination of the several systems or modes of pointing; tangent sights, and determination of their values; penetration and shock of projectiles, when used against wood, earth, or stone, and with direct and ricochet fire; recoil, and how affected by preponderance and position of trunnions in relation to axis of the gun.

Third branch—Naval tactics.—The different orders of steaming and sailing fleets, divisions, and squadrons, to be observed for battle and for other purposes; modes of forming such orders; of changing from one order to another; of reforming orders when disturbed by changes of wind; of interchanging and changing the position of different squadrons or divisions forming parts of a fleet; advantages of the different prescribed orders for general or special service; the leading objects to be kept in view in the arrangement of vessels of different strength or force for lines of battle, and in determining upon the manner of making or receiving an attack at sea and at anchor; examination of the best accounts of fleet actions; consideration of the advantages or defects of the plans of attack and defense, and of the execution of the details by the commanders of fleets, divisions, squadrons, and vessels; mode of communication by signals, embracing the naval code, the army code, and the commercial code.

Fourth branch—Infantry tactics.—Organization and formation of squad, company, and battalion; facing and wheeling; marching in line and by flank, and filing; manual of small arms; firing; charging; forming column in mass at half and at full distance, and reforming into line; extension and closing of column; column of route; reducing and increasing front; passage of defiles; advancing and retreating by flank, center, and in line; passage of obstacles; changes of front; forming and reducing square; exercise as skirmishers.

Fifth branch—Naval artillery.—School of the piece and school of the battery.

Sixth branch—The art of defense.—Fencing, small and broad sword; boxing and swimming.

Seventh branch—Naval construction.—Elements of naval architecture.

SECOND DEPARTMENT—MATHEMATICS.

First branch—A review of arithmetic.—The principles and practice of operations in hole numbers and in vulgar and decimal fractions; proportions; computation of perentage and interest; involution and evolution of numbers.

Algebra.—Fundamental operations; reduction and solution of equations of the first nd second degrees; reduction and transformation of fractional and surd quantities; roportions and progressions; summation of series; nature and construction of ogarithms.

Second branch—Geometry.—Plane and solid.

Third branch—Trigonometry.—Analytical investigation of trigonometrical formulas, and their application to the solution of all the cases in plane and spherical trigonometry; the construction and use of trigonometrical tables.

Fourth branch—Application of algebra and trigonometry to the mensuration of planes and solids.

Fifth branch—Descriptive geometry.—(The graphic illustration and solution of problems in solid geometry, and the application of this method, particularly to) the projections of the sphere.

Sixth branch—Analytical geometry.—Construction of algebraic expressions; solution of determinate problems; equations of the right line, plane and conic sections; [discussion of the general equations of the second degree, involving two or three variables; determination of loci; principal problems relating to the cylinder, cone, sphere, and spheroids.]

Seventh branch—[Differential and integral calculus.—Its principles and its application to maxima and minima, and the simpler problems relating to curves.]

THIRD DEPARTMENT—STEAM ENGINERY.

First branch—Mechanical drawing.—Application of right-line drawing and descriptive geometry to the making of drawings of marine steam machinery after construction.

Second branch—Heat.—Application of heat to steam, and the operation and conservation of marine engines and boilers.

Third branch—Steam.—Physical properties of water; method of generating steam; boiling points of fresh and sea water; measure of steam by atmospheres and mercurial column; steam distinguished from other elastic fluids; pressure, density, and temperture of steam; superheated steam; forms of instruments used to determine temperature and pressure of steam.

Fourth branch—Marine boilers.—General description of marine boilers—their peculiarities; details of construction; advantages and disadvantages of each type; methods of operating; appurtenances and instruments used in connection with marine boilers to determine their efficiency; means used for their proper care and preservation; economy of fuel and prevention of smoke.

Fifth branch—Marine engines.—General description of marine steam engines now in use—condensing and non-condensing; elementary parts of the steam engine; engines used for marine propulsion in the navy—advantages and disadvantages of each; detail parts of a marine engine—their use and conservation; different types of paddle-wheels and screw propellers; comparative efficiency of each for naval purposes; method of hoisting and coupling the screw and paddle-wheel—radial and feathering; duties to steam machinery when at sea and in port; repairing damages during and after an action; precautions against fire and spontaneous combustion, bad weather, and probability of an engagement; routine duties of the fire and engine rooms when under steam; coal bunkers and coaling ship; hints regarding selection of coal on foreign stations.

Sixth branch—Practical exercises.—Practical exercises; operating marine engines and boilers under steam; use of indicator and interpretation of its diagrams; practical observation of the methods of adjustment, and means used to insure the safety and preservation of marine machinery.

Seventh branch—Chemistry.—The practical application of chemistry to the combustion of fuel; corrosion of the metals; analysis of different kinds of fuel, sea water, boiler scale, lubricating matter, and illuminating oils.

This branch will be taught by lectures and experiment when marine boilers and engines are under discussion.

FOURTH DEPARTMENT—ASTRONOMY, NAVIGATION, AND SURVEYING.

First branch—Astronomy.—Descriptive and physical astronomy; description of the solar system; figure and magnitude of the earth, its motions and consequent changes of seasons; length of day and night; trade and periodical winds; nature and effects of parallax, refraction, dip of the horizon, precession, nutation, and aberration; theory of gravitation; Kepler's laws; explanation of the apparent motions of the sun, moon, planets, and comets, and the principles upon which the determination of their orbits depends; the moon's motions and phases; general theory of the tides; theory of eclipses; general description of the stars, and their distribution in space; measures of time; equation of time.

Second branch—Practical astronomy.—Including the use of astronomical instruments in determining the positions of celestial objects, and terrestrial latitudes and longitudes; optical principles involved in the construction of astronomical instruments, and in the theory of astronomical refraction. [Calculation of eclipses and occultations.]

Third branch—Navigation.—Sailing by compass; sailing on a great circle; various methods for finding a ship's place at sea; construction and use of charts, including topographical and hydrographic drawing; principles and use of the sextant and circle of reflection, and application of the glass prism to these instruments; the artificial horizon; the azimuth compass; methods of ascertaining the deviation of the compass, produced by local attraction on shipboard; the log, and other instruments for determining a ship's rate of sailing; sounding instruments; nature and use of the Nautical Almanac; relations of time under different meridians; computation of altitudes and azimuths of celestial objects; finding, by means of amplitudes and azimuths, the variations of the compass; finding the latitude by meridian observations of the sun, moon, planets, and stars; by observations near the meridian, by single altitudes at a given time, and by two altitudes of the same or different objects; finding the longitude by the chronometer, by lunar distances and by altitudes of the moon; Sumner's method of finding a line of position, and determining the ship's place by two such lines; rating a chronometer on shore by single altitudes, and by equal altitudes; and finding its error at sea by a series of lunar observations. Theory of the various problems of navigation and nautical astronomy, and the application of spherical trigonometry to thei solution; [consideration of the true figure of the earth, and the corrections in nautica problems depending upon it.]

Fourth branch—Surveying.—Its principles and practice; measurement of heights an distances; leveling; trigonometrical surveying; hydrographical surveying; direc measurement of a base line; measurement by sound; running lines of soundings reduction for tides; survey of a harbor or river; fixing the position of shoals, &c. running survey of a coast; [geodetic corrections in extended surveys;] application o astronomical observations for azimuth, latitude, and longitude.

FIFTH DEPARTMENT—NATURAL AND EXPERIMENTAL PHILOSOPHY.

First branch—Mechanics of solids.—Forces and equilibrium; composition and resolu tion of forces; uniform and varied motion; motion of projectiles in vacuo, and in resisting medium; center of gravity; equilibrium of a system of bodies; motion o translation of a body or system; motion and equilibrium about an axis; central forces falling bodies; pendulum and ballistic pendulum; laws of the planetary motions; effect of friction and adhesion, and of stiffness of cordage; mechanical powers; collision of bodies.

Second branch—Mechanics of liquids.—Mechanical properties of fluids; laws of equilibrium and pressure; flotation of bodies; stability and oscillation of floating bodies; specific gravity; [motion of liquids.]

Third branch—Mechanics of aëriform fluids.—Air-pump; weight and pressure of the atmosphere; laws of pressure; density and temperature; barometer; pumps; syphon; motion of elastic fluids.

Fourth branch—Acoustics.—Theory of waves in general; velocity of sound in different media; [molecular displacement; interference of waves;] reflection and echo; speaking and hearing trumpets; [vibrations of strings, of columns of air, and of plates and bells; communication of vibrations.]

Fifth branch—Optics.—General properties of light; catoptrics; dioptries; chromatics; vision; optical instruments; [physical optics.]

Sixth branch—Electricity.—Statical electricity; voltaic electricity; magnetism; electro-magnetism; thermo-electricity.

Seventh branch—Heat.—Conditions of heat; characteristics of heat; theories of heat, ancient and modern; sources of heat, conduction, radiation, and convection; specific heat; sensible and insensible caloric; effects of heat; instruments used for the measurement of heat; thermo-dynamics.

Eighth branch—Chemistry.—Chemical physics; general principles of chemical philosophy; principal elements and their compounds, especially as illustrating combustion, corrosion, the metals, analysis of fuels, water, sea water, boiler scale, lubricating matter, and illuminating oils.

SIXTH DEPARTMENT—ETHICS AND ENGLISH STUDIES.

First branch—English grammar.—Orthography; etymology; the analysis and synthesis of sentences; idioms; punctuation.

Second branch—Descriptive geography.—Knowledge of the land and water surface; the grand divisions of the earth, and their relative situation; extent and boundaries of the several countries in each of the grand divisions; their natural productions; their commerce, manufactures, and governments; their naval and military strength. The use of globes and maps.

Third branch—Physical geography.—The form and motions of the earth; the seasons and climates; the distribution of land and water; mountain ranges; declivities and basins; desert and lake zones; river systems; the currents of the ocean; geographical distribution of plants and animals; influence of physical causes on man.

Fourth branch—Outlines of history.—Ancient and modern; in the latter, mainly that of America, England, France, and Spain, during the last three centuries; written biographical and historical exercises.

Fifth branch—Rhetoric.—Verbal criticism; the principles of taste, and their application; original compositions, embracing official reports.

Sixth branch—Ethics.—The ground of moral obligation; our relations to God, and consequent duties; personal duties; the chief relations of men to each other in society, and the duties thence arising. (To be taught by means of familiar lectures, given by the chaplain.)

Seventh branch—Political science.—A review of the origin and structure of the federal government of the United States of America; its constitutional law; the acts of Congress for the better government of the navy; the law of nations generally; the rights and duties of nations in peace and in war.

SEVENTH DEPARTMENT—FRENCH.

Reading and writing the French language correctly; exercises in speaking it.

EIGHTH DEPARTMENT—SPANISH.

Reading and writing the Spanish language correctly; exercises in speaking it.

NINTH DEPARTMENT—DRAWING.

Right-lino drawing, sketching, and prospective; topographical and chart drawing.

The foregoing studies shall be distributed into four annual courses, and the midshipmen shall be arranged in four classes, each class pursuing one of these courses.

LETTER TO CANDIDATES.

NAVY DEPARTMENT,
Washington, January 31, 1863.

Application having been made on your behalf for admission to the United States Naval Academy, you will find, in the inclosed permit, a statement of the requisite qualifications for admission. Should you, on examination, show a fair proficiency in the branches of knowledge there indicated, and comply with the other conditions, you will be received as a midshipman, and become thenceforward an officer of the navy of the United States. So great is the importance of this step, not merely to yourself, but to the public, that the Secretary deems it a fit occasion to call your attention to the obligations which you assume in this new and honorable character.

You will bear in mind, then, that the government, in receiving you into its Naval Academy, undertakes to furnish you, at the public expense, with a superior scientific and practical education, under the instruction of thoroughly accomplished teachers. This is a privilege which, in the nature of things, can fall to the lot of but a small portion of the youth of the country, and it is one which, in all probability, many of the pupils of the Academy would otherwise not enjoy. It is, however, but the smallest part of what the government does for you. In admitting you to the Academy it secures to you an adequate provision, in a most honorable calling, for your future support, of which, while you live, nothing but incapacity or misconduct can deprive you. This great benefit, however, is not conferred on the pupils of the Naval Academy from any favoritism to them, but from great public motives. In the present state of the world the safety and honor of a country require that a portion of the young men should be regularly educated and trained in the science and art of war. This is necessary in both arms of the service, but peculiarly so in the navy. There are several instances in the land service of brilliant success on the part of chieftains who first entered the field in middle life; but the instances are much less frequent of distinguished naval commanders who did not commence their preparation in youth. This is the important reason for which the country has called the pupils of the Academy from their homes, and conferred upon them the above-mentioned enviable privileges.

You must, therefore, bear constantly in mind that these privileges, great as they are, are trusts for which the country will hold you strictly accountable. Henceforward, your time is not your own; it belongs to the public. The government takes you into its service in your youth because your preparation for the active duties of your career cannot be safely delayed to more advanced years. So much scientific, mechanical, and practical knowledge must be acquired, that nothing short of diligent application, commenced in early life, will enable the faithful officer to obtain a thorough mastery of his profession. It is a great error to suppose that nothing is necessary to make a good officer but the physical courage required in time of action, and which is to some extent a natural gift. This, of course, is indispensable; but it is one only of the qualifications for the service. Beginning at the foundation, the thorough-bred naval officer must know something of ship-building, alike in wood and iron ; not that he needs the knowledge of the naval architect, but he must be able to judge of the work both of construction and repair, and be competent to provide a prompt remedy for disasters at sea. He must be intimately acquainted with the rig, equipment, and handling of his vessel ; must understand the navigation of the ocean by sails and steam ; be familiar with the great currents of the sea and of the atmosphere; and have an accurate knowledge of the principal ports and harbors in every quarter of the globe. He must be thoroughly versed in every variety of naval armament, ordnance, and ammunition—a field of knowledge of which the limits have been greatly enlarged of late years, and in which still further advances are in rapid progress. Thus prepared in the lower branches of his profession, he must, by experience, gradually acquired on a small scale, and by diligent study of the lives and exploits of illustrious commanders, learn, as far as it can be learned in this way, not only how single ships are fought, but how great fleets are maneuvered and led to glorious victories.

To attain these great ends, abstract science and mechanical art furnish but the lower instruments. Moral influences must lend their all-powerful aid. Beginning with the arduous task of self-government, of which the habit must be acquired by cheerful conformity to the discipline of the Academy and the subordination of the service, the accomplished officer must learn the great art of governing others over whom he may be placed in the public service. He must learn the lesson of command in the school of obedience. A fractions and intractable pupil, if he succeed in obtaining promotion, will be nearly sure to make an arbitrary and tyrannical officer. Treated, as you will be, with parental kindness at the Academy, nothing that you will learn there is more important than the art of gaining the confidence and winning the affection of those whom you may hereafter command. The officer who acquires the good will of his men by kind words and deeds will be far more successful in enforcing the necessarily strict discipline of a man-of-war than one who deals in rough language, oaths, and harsh treatment. It is related of a distinguished British naval officer, (Lord Collingwood,) that the most refractory seamen were transferred to his vessel from all the other ships in the fleet, not because his discipline was the most severe, but because it was at once the most gentle and the most efficacious.

The duties thus enumerated, numerous and important as they are, are not all that devolve on the naval officer. In addition to the skill appropriately belonging to his profession, it is necessary that his manners should be marked with courtesy and refinement, and that his mind should be amply stored with useful knowledge. In the service of a great naval power, he will, on foreign stations, often be called upon to appear as the representative of his government. He will be brought into contact with the nava commanders of other countries, and sometimes with personages of the highest ran and consequence. On these occasions the good name and consideration of his countr are, to some extent, in his hands. Still more, he will sometimes be obliged, with littl opportunity for deliberation, and no time to consult his government, to decide import ant questions of the law of nations. It is evident that the most momentous con sequences may flow from the degree of intelligence with which he may act on suc occasions.

These are the reasons for which the country calls a select number of her children, i the morning of their days, to enter her naval service. The common parent of all, sh bestows upon them these enviable advantages in order to fit them for the various an arduous duties to which I have alluded. The young officer, accordingly, when h enters the Naval Academy, becomes the pledged servant of the country, of the whol country, bound by the strongest ties of duty and gratitude to serve her with fidelit and zeal. He is henceforward an officer, not of the State in which he was born or i which he resides, but of the United States of America. He may have been born at th East or the West, the North or the South, but his allegiance is due to the Union—t the government which has educated him, which has commissioned him, and which h has solemnly sworn to defend. Wheresoever the voice of duty or lawful authorit may call him, there he will cheerfully hasten to sustain the honor of his country's flag to protect her lawful commerce, to combat her enemies. It may be his duty to risk perhaps to sacrifice, his life, like the naval heroes who shed undying glory on th American Navy in the last generation, in open war against a legitimate foe; or t follow a piratical sea-rover, meanly fitted out by foreign cupidity for the work o devastation and plunder; or to pass weary days and nights in watching the ports o rebels in arms against their country; or to launch the terrific thunders of his broad sides on their fortresses—whatever the duty may be, it will be diligently, zealously and heroically performed.

The character of the struggle in which the government and loyal people of the country have been engaged gives a peculiar significance to these considerations; nor can the Secretary forbear to allude to the all-important services which were rendered by the navy during that contest. The outbreak of the rebellion found this arm of the service on a peace establishment, its squadrons widely dispersed; some of its most important home stations situated in the seceding States, and soon seized—too often with treacherous connivance—and passed into rebel hands. Enfeebled as the navy was by these causes, and still further by the necessary sacrifice of vessels to prevent them from falling into the hands of the enemy; compelled to call into the service with urgent haste a numerous fleet of vessels not constructed for warlike purposes; above all, obliged, without previous preparation, to inaugurate a novel system of armature, the navy performed its herculean labors with an energy and success that reflect the highest credit on all belonging to it, officers and men, and which the Secretary takes great pleasure in holding up to the emulation of the young men at the Academy, who will hereafter be called upon to sustain the well-earned reputation of this branch of the service.

Especially let the young men now entering the navy impress upon their minds, as the great lesson of the day, that of all the duties of a faithful officer, the first and foremost is that of fidelity to his flag—the sacred symbol of the government which has trained him to its defense and confided its honor to his keeping. Let him, as he sets his foot on the threshold of the Academy, form the firm resolve, living or dying, to be faithful to that great trust. Let him, in advance, steel his mind against the wretched sophistry under the influence of which a portion of the naval officers in the rebellious States, (but by no means all of them,) deceived and misled, against their own better impulses, by the craft of politicians, have allowed themselves to raise a parricidal arm against their country, employing the fruits of the education received at its expense, and of the experience gained in its service, in aid of an unprovoked and cruel rebellion. Before he enters on actual service, the young officer takes a solemn oath "to support, protect, and defend the Constitution of the United States against all enemies, whether domestic or foreign;" and the Secretary would earnestly impress upon the young men, on their admission to the Naval Academy, that no human power can absolve them from that obligation. The madness of the hour may cause a misguided man to forget that he has called his God so to deal with him as he shall keep or break his oath, but the time will come, even in this world, when the sin of perjury will lie heavy on his soul.

But the Secretary is confident that no one of the young gentlemen now entering the Naval Academy, or already there, will ever incur the foul reproach of betraying the flag of the Union. They will uphold it on every sea and on every shore, by every effort and at every hazard, in the storm of the elements or the storm of battle. They will live for it and fight for it; if need be, they will bleed for it. While it floats they will stand by it, and, if it must sink, they will go down with it, rather than disgrace or betray it.

The Secretary forbears to enter into any particular statements as to the studies, exercises, and discipline of the Academy. The intelligent officer charged with the superintendence of the institution, and who possesses the entire confidence of the department, aided by his able and efficient associates, will from time to time call your attention to the various details of duty; and the Secretary confidently trusts that, under their guidance, you will, by the faithful improvement of your great opportunities, prepare yourself for eminent usefulness and high honor in the service of the country.

GIDEON WELLES,
Secretary of the Navy.

REGULATIONS

THE ADMISSION OF CANDIDATES INTO THE NAVAL ACADEMY.

I. The number of midshipmen allowed at the Academy is one for every member and elegate of the House of Representatives, one for the District of Columbia, ten appointed annually at large, and ten selected each year from boys enlisted in the navy ho have been at least one year in the service on board a naval vessel.

II. The nomination of candidates for admission from the District of Columbia, from he enlisted boys, and at large, is made by the President. The nomination of a candidate from any congressional district or Territory is made on the recommendation of the member or delegate, from actual residents of his district or Territory.

III. Each year, as soon after the fifth of March as possible, members and delegates will be notified, in writing, of vacancies that may exist in their districts. If such members or delegates neglect to recommend candidates by the first of July in that year, the Secretary of the Navy is required by law to fill the vacancies existing in districts actually represented in Congress.

IV. The nomination of candidates is made annually, between the fifth of March and the first of July. Candidates who are nominated in time to enable them to reach the Academy between the twentieth and thirtieth of June, will receive permission to present themselves at that time to the Superintendent of the Naval Academy for examination as to their qualifications for admission. Those who are nominated prior to July 1st, but not in time to attend the June examination, will be examined between the twentieth and thirtieth of September following; and should any candidate fail to report, or be found physically or mentally disqualified for admission in June, the member or delegate from whose district he was nominated will be notified to recommend another candidate, who shall be examined between the twentieth and thirtieth of September following.

V. No candidate will be admitted into the Naval Academy unless he shall have passed a satisfactory examination before the Academic Board, and is found (in the opinion of a medical board, to be composed of the surgeon of the Naval Academy and two other medical officers designated by the Secretary of the Navy) physically sound, well formed, and of robust constitution, and qualified to endure the arduous labors of an officer in the navy.

VI. Candidates for appointment as midshipmen must be between fourteen and eighteen years of age when examined for admission. All candidates for admission will be required to certify, *on honor*, to their precise age, to the Academic Board, previous to examination, and none will be examined who are over or under the prescribed age. They must be of good moral character, satisfactory testimonials of which, from persons of good repute in the neigborhood of their respective residences, must be presented; and testimonials from clergymen, instructors in colleges and high schools, will have special weight. They must also pass a satisfactory examination before the Academic Board in reading, writing, spelling, arithmetic, geography, and English grammar, viz: in *reading*, they must read clearly and intelligibly from any English narrative work— as, for example, Bancroft's History of the United States; in *writing* and *spelling*, they must write from dictation, in a legible hand, and spell with correctness both orally and in writing; in *arithmetic*, they will be examined in numeration and the addition, subtraction, multiplication, and division of whole numbers and vulgar and decimal fractions, and in proportion, or the rule of three; in *geography*, they will be examined as to the leading grand divisions—the continents, oceans, and seas, the chief mountains and rivers, and the boundaries and population of the chief nations, their government, capitals, and chief cities; in *English grammar*, they will be examined as to the parts of speech and the elementary construction of sentences, and will be required to write an original paragraph of a few sentences. The Board will judge whether the proficiency of the candidate in these branches is sufficient to qualify him to enter upon the studies of the Academy.

VII. Any one of the following conditions will be sufficient to reject a candidate:

Feeble constitution; permanently impaired general health; decided cachexia; all chronic diseases, or results of injuries that would permanently impair efficiency, viz:

1. Infectious disorders.
2. Weak or disordered intellect.
3. Unnatural curvature of spine.
4. Epilepsy, or other convulsion, within five years.
5. Chronic impaired vision, or chronic disease of the organs of vision.
6. Great permanent hardness of hearing, or chronic disease of the ears.
7. Loss or decay of teeth to such an extent as to interfere with digestion and impair health.
8. Impediment of speech to such an extent as to impair efficiency in the performance of duty.
9. Decided indications of liability to pulmonary disease.
10. Permanent inefficiency of either of the extremities.
11. Hernia.
12. Incurable sarcocele, hydrocele, fistula, stricture, or hemorrhoids.
13. Large varicose veins of lower limbs. Chronic ulcers.
14. Attention will also be paid to the stature of the candidate; and no one *manifestly* under-sized for his age will be received into the Academy. In case of doubt about the physical condition of the candidate, any marked deviation from the usual standard of height will add materially to the consideration for rejection.

NOTE.—The Medical Board of 1864 adopted the following standard for the height of candidates: 14 years of age, 4 feet 10 inches; 15 years, 5 feet; 16 years, 5 feet 2 inches; 17 years, 5 feet 3 inches; 18 years, (nearly,) 5 feet 4 inches; the candidates to be of proportionate size, especially with regard to cerebral, osseous, and muscular development; the youngest to weigh not less than 100 pounds, and the oldest not less than 120 pounds.

15. The Board will exercise a proper discretion in the application of the above conditions to each case; rejecting no candidate who is likely to be efficient in the service, and admitting no one who is likely to prove physically inefficient.

VIII. If both these examinations result favorably, the candidate will receive an appointment as midshipman, become an inmate of the Academy, and be allowed his actual and necessary traveling expenses from his residence to the Naval Academy, and be required to sign articles by which he will bind himself to serve in the United States Navy eight years, (including his term of probation at the Naval Academy,) unless sooner discharged. If, on the contrary, he shall not pass both of these examinations, he will receive neither an appointment nor his traveling expenses, nor can he by law have the privilege of another examination for admission to the same class unless recommended by the board of examiners.

IX. When candidates shall have passed the required examinations, and been admitted as members of the Academy, they must immediately furnish themselves with the following articles, viz:

Two navy blue uniform suits;	Six pair of socks;
One fatigue suit;	Four pair of drawers;
Two navy blue uniform caps;	Six pocket handkerchiefs;
One uniform overcoat;	One black silk handkerchief or stock;
Six white shirts;	One mattress;

One pillow;
One pair of blankets;
One bed cover, or spread;
Two pair of sheets;
Four pillow-cases;
Six towels;
Two pair of shoes or boots;

One hair-brush;
One tooth-brush;
One clothes-brush;
One coarse comb for the hair;
One fine comb for the hair;
One tumbler, or mug; and
One thread and needle case.

Room-mates will jointly procure, for their common use, one looking-glass, one wash-asin, one water-pail, one slop-bucket, and one broom. These articles may be obtained om the storekeeper of the Academy, of good quality and at fair prices.

X. Each midshipman must, on admission, deposit with the paymaster the sum of one undred dollars, for which he will be credited on the books of that officer, to be ex-ended by direction of the Superintendent for the purchase of text-books and other uthorized articles besides those enumerated in the preceding article.

XI. A midshipman found deficient at any examination cannot, by law, be continued t the Academy or in the service, unless upon the recommendation of the Academic oard.

XII. A midshipman who voluntarily resigns his appointment within a year of the ime of his admission to the Academy will be required to refund the amount paid him or traveling expenses.

XIII. A midshipman may be advanced to any class which he may be found qualified o join, either upon his admission or at any subsequent examination; and he may be graduated at any June examination at which he shall be found fully qualified to pass a graduating academic examination.

GIDEON WELLES,
Secretary of the Navy.

3 N A

OFFICERS AND MIDSHIPMEN

ATTACHED TO THE

PRACTICE SHIPS SAVANNAH, MACEDONIAN, AND DALE—SUMMER CRUISE, 1869.

Captain N. B. HARRISON, *Commanding the Division.*

SLOOP SAVANNAH.

Lieut. Commanders—C. L. Franklin, J. F. McGlensey, G. W. Coffin, F. A. Cook, and S. H. Baker. *Lieutenants*—W. W. Mead and T. P. Wilson. *Surgeon*—J. McMaster. *Assistant Surgeon*—F. K. Hartzell. *Paymaster*—W. F. A. Torbert. *Assistant Professors*—John M. Rice and Jules Leroux. *Boatswain*—P. J. Miller. *Gunner*—T. P. Venable. *Carpenter*—W. H. Rickards. *Sailmaker*—J. J. Stanford.

FIRST CLASS OF MIDSHIPMEN.

W. S. Baker.	M. D. Hyde.	J. B. Milton.	N. Sargent.
J. L. Carter.	J. D. Keeler.	J. B. Murdock.	J. H. Sawyers.
J. B. Collins.	F. L. Ludlow.	H. C. Nye.	H. W. Schaefer.
M. C. Dimock.	C. H. Lyman.	R. G. Peck.	T. C. Spencer.
H. F. Fickbohm.	C. McDonald.	H. R. Penington.	J. H. Utley.
F. Gentsch.	A. McCrackin.	C. P. Rees.	W. H. Van de Carr.
S. L. Graham.	G. W. Mentz.	W. Remsen.	C. E. Vreeland.
L. C. Heilner.	G. A. Merriam.	T. G. C. Salter.	F. Winslow.
G. W. Holman.			

SECOND CLASS.

W. C. Babcock.	W. P. Elliott.	F. W. Nabor.	C. Thomas.
A. C. Baker.	C. A. Foster.	T. S. Plunket.	B. C. Tillinghast.
C. W. Bartlett.	W. S. French.	G. A. Sanderson.	F. B. Veazie.
C. Bruns.	F. Guertin.	S. Seabury.	A. Ward.
P. Busbee.	F. S. Hotchkin.	W. H. Slack.	D. Whipple.
A. J. Dabney.	J. L. Hunsicker.	S. A. Staunton.	J. M. Wight.
J. Downes.	H. McCrea.	R. D. Stevens.	D. L. Wilson.
J. T. Edson.	H. P. McIntosh.		

THIRD CLASS.

D. F. Baker.	R. H. Fletcher.	N. T. James.	W. Polmyer.
J. A. Barber.	C. E. Fox.	O. E. Lasher.	B. F. Rinehart.
C. H. Crosswait.	J. C. Fremont.	O. W. Lowry.	A. C. Thompson.
J. G. Dieterich.	W. H. Garrett.	C. H. Lyeth.	F. Tyler.
A. V. Dockery.	G. W. Hey.	J. Medary.	G. B. Vandervoort.

FOURTH CLASS.

D. R. Keeler.   W. M. Slough.   Total, 85.

SLOOP MACEDONIAN.

Commander—J. S. Skerrett. *Lieut. Commanders*—J. A. Howell, W. T. Sampson, B. J. Cromwell, C. F. Blake, P. F. Harrington, and F. Pearson. *Master*—William Watts. *Surgeon*—H. C. Nelson. *Assistant Surgeon*—M. C. Drennen. *Paymaster*—F. H. Swan. *Chaplain*—D. McLaren. *Assistant Professor*—L. F. Prud'homme. *Boatswain*—William Jones. *Gunner*—John Gaskins. *Carpenter*—Benjamin R. Murphy. *Sailmaker*—John W. North.

FIRST CLASS OF MIDSHIPMEN.

J. S. Abbot.	G. L. Dyer.	W. S. Holliday.	W. P. Ray.
C. Briggs.	F. Ellery.	E. M. Hughes.	L. L. Reamey.
J. H. Bull.	C. F. Emmerich.	J. J. Hunker.	C. S. Richman.
G. A. Calhoun.	J. M. Gore.	H. M. Jacoby.	H. O. Rittenhouse.
W. P. Conway.	H. L. Green.	L. P. Juett.	H. R. Tyler.
F. H. Crosby.	H. Harris.	B. Leach.	M. F. Wright.
J. W. Danenhower.	J. Hubbard.	A. B. Milliman.	

SECOND CLASS.

H. H. Barroll.	J. C. Cresap.	W. M. Irwin.	J. E. Roller.
J. C. Burnett.	J. H. Fraunces.	F. H. Lefavor.	B. B. Scott.
C. G. Calkins.	J. C. Freeman.	W. H. E. Masser.	W. E. Sewell.
A. H. Cobb.	C. D. Galloway.	W. A. Marshall.	T. C. Wood.
W. P. Clason.	F. E. Greene.	E. F. Qualtrough.	G. A. Vail.
A. A. Crandall.	G. C. Hanus.		

THIRD CLASS.

V. L. Cottman.	C. T. Mitchell.	W. T. B. O'Reilly.	W. H. H. Sutherland.
A. T. Freeman.	C. R. Miles.	J. M. Roper.	H. S. Waring.
R. H. Galt.	A. Mertz.	F. E. Sawyer.	J. H. Winlock.
W. C. Heacock.	F. H. Powers.	M. K. Schwenk.	G. T. Winston.
R. H. McLean.			

FOURTH CLASS.

T. F. Dixon.   R. S. Graham.   J. Y. Oliver.   T. E. D. W. Veeder.

Total, 70.

SLOOP DALE.

Lieut. Commanders—Edward Terry, S. Casey, H. F. Picking, W. C. Wise, and W. B. Hoff. *Master*—F. H. Sheppard. *Past Assistant Surgeon*—E. C. Ver Meulen. *Boatswain*—William Long. *Gunner*—George Fouse.

FIRST CLASS OF MIDSHIPMEN.

J. P. J. Augur.	W. Kilburn.	W. G. Mayer.	T. Porter.
A. C. Dillingham.	C. P. Kunhardt.	H. Osterhaus.	W. M. Wood.

FOURTH CLASS.

. S. Arnold.	J. R. Dexter.	S. C. Lemly.	H. J. Rodman.
. J. Axson.	H. C. Fales.	J. S. Manley.	W. H. Schuetze.
. J. Badger.	F. A. Fenn.	A. A. Michelson.	M. A. Shufeldt.
. W. Bean.	G. Fowler.	F. J. Milligan.	J. Smith.
. W. Blakely.	H. W. Greenough.	H. Morrell.	R. D. Strong.
. W. Burns.	C. F. Holder.	J. O. Nicholson.	W. V. B. Topping.
. L. Case.	T. B. Howard.	G. L. North.	E. B. Underwood.
7. N. Coret.	F. T. Jenkins.	H. C. Pell.	J. P. Underwood.
7. H. Craig.	J. P. Johnson.	C. F. Putnam.	F. C. C. Van Vliet.
. W. Danner.	J. S. Jouett.	E. Raines.	F. A. Wilner.
. W. Deering.	A. M. Knight.	J. M. Robinson.	L. Yound.

Total, 52.

Officers attached to the following vessels:

CONSTITUTION—(SECOND RATE.)

Lieut. Com'r GEORGE DEWEY, *in charge of vessels.*
Paymaster—Worthington Goldsborough. *Chaplain*—Henry B. Hibben. *Mates*—Joseph odgers, Frederick Miller, William G. Smith, and Roscoe V. Wickes.

GUNNERY-SHIP SANTEE—(SECOND RATE.)

Mates—Robert Robinson, Charles H. Chase, Lewis M. Melcher.

PRACTICE-SHIP DALE—(FOURTH RATE.)

Boatswain—William Long.

PRACTICE-SHIP MARION—(FOURTH RATE.)

Boatswain—Jeremiah Harding. *Mates*—Robert Silver, Charles J. Murphy, and William J. Best.

AMPHITRITE, (IRON CLAD, THIRD RATE.)

Second Assistant Engineer John Bosthwick, *in charge of machinery afloat.*

MERCURY—(STEAM TUG.)

Mate John Brown, *in charge.*

PHLOX—(STEAM TENDER.)

Mate Benjamin G. Perry, *in charge.*
Mate—Lewis Burns.

SCHOONER AMERICA.

WYANDANK—(FOURTH RATE.)

PRACTICE-SHIP MACEDONIAN—(SECOND RATE.)

Paymaster—Francis H. Swan.

PRACTICE-SHIP SAVANNAH—(THIRD RATE.)

COURSE OF INSTRUCTION FOR ENGINEER CLASS.

(ACTING THIRD ASSISTANTS.)

Mechanical Drawing.—*a*, Elements; *b*, Details and plans of machines.

Physics.—*a*, Heat; *b*, Steam.

Chemistry.—*a*, Chemical philosophy; *b*, Elements; *c*, Analysis—qualitative and blow pipe; *d*, Coals, ores, and oils—lubricating and illuminating.

Thermo-dynamics.

Machines.—*a*, Cinematics; *b*, Theory of machines; *c*, Prime movers—Hydraulic motors steam-engines, air-engines, electro-magnetic motors; *d*, Construction of machines; *e* Location and erection of machines; *f*, Designs and estimates for, and reviews of, specia machines.

Construction.—*a*, Plans and estimates for boiler and machine shops, foundries, smeltin₍ works, and rolling mills; *b*, Plans and estimates for ships' ways and slips.

Management of Machinery.—Practical exercises with steam engine and boilers.

Iron Ship-building.—*a*, Designing and construction; *b*, Inspection; *c*, Launching an₍ repairs.

Practical Exercises.—Personal manipulations of tools used in working woods an₍ metals.

REGULATIONS

HE APPOINTMENT OF CADET ENGINEERS IN THE NAVY.

I. In pursuance of the third and fourth sections of an act passed at the first session of the 38th Congress, approved July 4, 1864, *"To authorize the Secretary of the Navy to rovide for the education of Naval Constructors and Steam Engineers, and for other purposes,"* and of the second section of an act passed at the first session of the 39th Congress, approved March 2, 1867, entitled *"An act to amend certain acts in relation to the Navy,"* applications will be received by the Navy Department for the appointment of cadet engineers.

II. The application is to be addressed to the Secretary of the Navy, and can be made by the candidate or by any person for him, and his name will be placed on the register. The registry of a name, however, gives no assurance of an appointment, and no preference will be given in the selection to priority of application.

III. The number of cadet engineers is limited by law to fifty. The candidate must be not less than eighteen nor more than twenty-two years of age, and his application must be accompanied by satisfactory evidence of moral character and health, with information regarding date of birth and educational advantages hitherto enjoyed. Candidates who receive permission will present themselves to the Superintendent of the Naval Academy between the 20th and 30th of September, for examination as to their qualifications for admission.

IV. The course of study will comprise two academic years. All cadets who graduate will be immediately warranted as third assistant engineers in the navy. The pay of a cadet is the same as that of midshipmen.

V. The academic examination previous to appointment will be on the following subjects, namely: *Arithmetic;* the candidate will be examined in numeration and the addition, subtraction, multiplication, and division of whole numbers, and of vulgar and decimal fractions; in reduction; in proportion, or rule of three, direct and inverse; and in involution and the extraction of square and cube roots. *Algebra,* (Bourdon;) *Geometry,* (Davies's Legendre;) Rudimentary *Natural Philosophy;* Elements of *Inorganic Chemistry;* English Grammar and English *Composition;* *History of the United States;* also, a brief outline of *Ancient* and *Modern History.* The candidate will also be required to exhibit a fair degree of proficiency in pencil sketching and right-line drawing, and he must be able to describe all the different parts of ordinary condensing and non-condensing engines, explain their uses and operation; also, the ordinary tools used for construction purposes.

VI. Any one of the following conditions will be sufficient to reject a candidate:

Feeble constitution; permanently impaired general health; decided cachexia; all chronic diseases, or results of injuries that would permanently impair efficiency, viz:

1. Infectious disorders.
2. Weak or disordered intellect.
3. Unnatural curvature of spine.
4. Epilepsy, or other convulsion, within five years.
5. Chronic impaired vision, or chronic diseases of the organs of vision.
6. Great permanent hardness of hearing, or chronic disease of the ears.
7. Loss or decay of teeth to such an extent as to interfere with digestion and impair health.

8. Impediment of speech to such an extent as to impair efficiency in the performance of duty.

9. Decided indications of liability to pulmonary disease.

10. Permanent inefficiency of either of the extremities.

11. Hernia.

12. Incurable sarcocele, hydrocele, fistula, stricture, or hemorrhoids.

13. Large varicose veins of lower limbs. Chronic ulcers.

14. Attention will also be paid to the stature of the candidate; and no one *manifestly* undersized for his age will be received into the Academy. In case of doubt about the physical condition of the candidate, any marked deviation from the usual standard of height will add materially to the consideration for rejection.

15. The Board will exercise a proper discretion in the application of the above conditions to each case ; rejecting no candidate who is likely to be efficient in the service, and admitting no one who is likely to prove physically inefficient.

VII. If both these examinations result favorably, the candidate will receive an appointment as a cadet engineer, become an inmate of the Academy, and be allowed his actual and necessary traveling expenses from his residence to the Naval Academy, and be required to sign articles by which he will bind himself to serve in the United States Navy six years, (including his term of probation at the Naval Academy,) unless sooner discharged. If, on the contrary, he shall not pass both of these examinations, he will receive neither an appointment nor his traveling expenses, nor can he have the privilege of another examination for admission *to the same class* unless recommended by the Board of Examiners.

VIII. When candidates shall have passed the required examinations and been admitted as members of the Academy, they must immediately furnish themselves with the following articles, viz :

One navy blue uniform suit ;	One bed cover or spread ;
One fatigue suit ;	Two pair of sheets ;
One navy blue uniform cap ;	Four pillow-cases ;
One uniform overcoat ;	Six towels ;
Six white shirts ;	Two pair of shoes or boots ;
Six pair of socks ;	One hair-brush ;
Four pair of drawers ;	One tooth-brush ;
Six pocket handkerchiefs ;	One clothes-brush ;
One black silk handkerchief, or stock ;	One coarse comb for the hair ;
One mattress ;	One fine comb for the hair ;
One pillow ;	One tumbler, or mug ; and
One pair of blankets ;	One thread and needle case.

Room-mates will jointly procure, for their common use, one looking-glass, one wash-basin, one water pail, one slop bucket, and one broom. These articles may be obtained from the storekeeper of the Academy, of good quality and at fair prices.

IX. Each cadet engineer must, on admission, deposit with the paymaster the sum of seventy-five dollars, for which he will be credited on the books of that officer, to be expended by direction of the Superintendent for the purchase of text-books and other authorized articles besides those enumerated in the preceding article.

X. While at the Academy the cadets will be examined, from time to time, according to the regulations prescribed by the Navy Department; and if found deficient at any examination, or dismissed for misconduct, they cannot, by law, be continued in the Academy or naval service, except upon recommendation of the Academic Board.

XI. A cadet engineer who voluntarily resigns his appointment will be required to refund the amount paid him for traveling expenses.

GIDEON WELLES,
Secretary of the Navy.

COURSE OF INSTRUCTION

FOR

CADET ENGINEERS AT THE UNITED STATES NAVAL ACADEMY.

MATHEMATICAL COURSE.

FIRST YEAR—FIRST TERM.

First branch—Trigonometry.—Analytical investigation of trigonometrical formulas, and their application to the solution of all the cases in plane trigonometry; the construction and use of trigonometrical tables.

Second branch—Application of algebra and trigonometry to the mensuration of planes and solids.

FIRST YEAR—SECOND TERM.

Third branch—Analytical geometry.—Construction of algebraic expressions; solution of determinate problems; equations of the right-line, plane, and conic sections, (discussion of the general equations of the second degree, involving two or three variables; determination of loci; principal problems relating to the cylinder, cone, sphere, and spheroids.)

SECOND YEAR—FIRST TERM.

Fourth branch—(Differential and integral calculus.—Its principles, and its application to maxima and minima, and simpler problems relating to curves.)

NOTE.—The examination for admission will require a very thorough knowledge of Bourdon's Algebra as far as the general theory of equation; also, of Davies' Legendre and mensuration.

Those who pass a satisfactory examination for admission, and can show proficiency in the more advanced studies of the department, will be assigned corresponding positions in the course. Those who show a sufficient acquaintance with *all* the mathematical branches taught at this institution, will at once be excused from further instruction in this department.

NAVAL ENGINEERING.

Mechanical Drawing.—a, Elements; *b,* Details and plans of machines.

Physics.—a, Heat; *b,* Steam.

Chemistry.—a, Chemical philosophy; *b,* Elements; *c,* Analysis—qualitative and blow-pipe; *d,* Coals, Ores, and Oils—lubricating and illuminating.

Thermo-dynamics.

Machines.—a, Cinematics; *b,* Theory of machines; *c,* Prime movers—Hydraulic motors, Steam engines, Air engines, Electro-magnetic motors; *d,* Construction of machines; *e,* Location and erection of machines; *f,* Designs and estimates for, and reviews of, special machines.

Construction.—a, Plans and estimates for boiler and machine shops, foundries, smelting works, and rolling mills; *b,* Plans and estimates for ships' ways and slips.

Management of machinery.—Practical exercises with steam engines and boilers.

Iron ship-building.—a, Designing and construction; *b,* Inspection; *c,* Launching and repairs.

Practical exercises.—Personal manipulation of tools used in working woods and metals.

FRENCH.

Reading and writing the French language correctly; exercises in speaking it.

SPANISH.

Reading and writing the Spanish language correctly; exercises in speaking it.

NON-PROFESSIONAL PRACTICAL EXERCISES.

Fencing and gymnastics.

4 N A

RESIGNATIONS, DISMISSALS, ETC.,

FROM

OCTOBER 1, 1868, TO SEPTEMBER 30, 1869, INCLUSIVE.

RESIGNATIONS.

Midshipman Edward L. Shaffer ....Oct. 13, 186£

Midshipman Montgomery Wilcox ....Oct. 13, 186£

Midshipman Edward R. Norton ....Nov. 13, 186£

Midshipman Henry H. Kirkpatrick.....:...............................Jan. 5, 186£

Midshipman Halsey McKie Wing...Jan. 7, 186£

Midshipman George B. Hoyt ....Jan. 22, 186£

Midshipman Henry E. Muhlenberg:......................................Jan. 28, 186£

Midshipman Thomas C. Denny..Feb. 3, 186£

Midshipman William A. Siter ....Feb. 3, 186£

Midshipman Harrington L. Gosling......................................Feb. 6, 186£

Midshipman William D. Rosencrantz ....Feb. 8, 186£

Midshipman Thomas Rodd..Feb. 13, 186£

Midshipman Robert J. Anderton ....Feb. 15, 186£

Midshipman Levi Fox ....Feb. 15, 186£

Midshipman Charles H. Brahe...Mar. 15, 186£

Midshipman Wisner G. Scott...Mar. 15, 186£

Midshipman Philip Arnold...Mar. 15, 186£

Midshipman Zachary T. Babcock..Mar. 15, 186£

Midshipman Thomas D. Carnahan .....:.................................Mar. 15, 186

Midshipman Walter Frazer ....Mar. 15, 186

Midshipman Franklin L. Greene ....Mar. 15, 186

Midshipman David S. Little ....Mar. 15, 186

Midshipman William S. Long ....Mar. 15, 186

Midshipman George D. McCarty .....:...................................Mar. 15, 186

Midshipman Dwight L. Worsley ....Mar. 15, 186

Midshipman William L. Baldwin...............................<:..Mar. 15, 186

Midshipman Abel B. Brown..Mar. 15, 186

Midshipman Joel H. Burns..Mar. 15, 186

Midshipman Edward Lloyd ....Mar. 15, 186

Midshipman Horace W. Mann...Mar. 24, 186

Midshipman Benjamin M. Shaffner ....Mar. 24, 186

Midshipman Eugene C. Tiltman...Mar. 24, 186

Midshipman John R. Spears ....April 9, 186

Midshipman Charles W. Brown ....April 9, 18

Midshipman Arthur C. Smith ....June 3, 186

Midshipman Albert B. Fowler...June 8, 186

Midshipman William S. King ....June 8, 18

Midshipman George A. Zabriskie..June 8, 18

Midshipman Gaspar C. Barnette ....:...............................June 8, 18

Midshipman Walter T. Livingston ....June 8, 18

Midshipman Jacob K. Nagle ....June 8, 18

Midshipman Alexander Kirkland...June 9, 18

Midshipman Lemuel Van Epps...June 9, 18

Midshipman James S. Manley..June 14, 18

Midshipman Thomas F. Dixon ....Sept. 29, 18

DISMISSALS, ETC.

Midshipman George W. Cory, dropped.................................Oct. 19, 1868.
Midshipman Henry L. Heiskell, dropped ....Oct. 19, 1868.
Midshipman Julian H. Brown, dismissed ....Feb. 8, 1869.
Midshipman Hiram Hancock, dropped................................Mar. 16, 1869.

Lightning Source UK Ltd.
Milton Keynes UK
UKHW020310261118
332889UK00007B/174/P

9 780265 207352